My World of Science

BENDY AND RIGID

Angela Royston

Heinemann
LIBRARY

www.heinemann.co.uk/library
Visit our website to find out more information about **Heinemann Library** books.

To order:
☎ Phone 44 (0) 1865 888066
📄 Send a fax to 44 (0) 1865 314091
💻 Visit the Heinemann Bookshop at www.heinemann.co.uk/library to browse our catalogue and order online.

First published in Great Britain by Heinemann Library, Halley Court, Jordan Hill, Oxford OX2 8EJ, part of Harcourt Education.

Heinemann is a registered trademark of Harcourt Education Ltd.

Editorial: Andrew Farrow and Dan Nunn
Design: Jo Hinton-Malivoire and
    Tinstar Design Limited (www.tinstar.co.uk)
Picture Research: Maria Joannou and Sally Smith
Production: Viv Hichens

Originated by Blenheim Colour Ltd
Printed and bound in China by
    South China Printing Company

ISBN 0 431 13728 5
07 06 05 04 03
10 9 8 7 6 5 4 3 2 1

British Library Cataloguing in Publication Data
Royston, Angela
Bendy and rigid. – (My world of science)
1. Flexure – Juvenile literature
I. Title
620.1'1244

A full catalogue record for this book is available from the British Library.

Acknowledgements
The publishers would like to thank the following for permission to reproduce photographs:
Chris Honeywell p. **26**; David Bradford p. **24**; Eye Ubiquitous pp. **9**, **29** (Chris Fairclough); Getty Images pp. **20**, **25**; Photodisc p. **17**; Powerstock Zefa p. **12**; Rupert Horrox p. **8**; Trevor Clifford pp. **4**, **5**, **6**, **7**, **10**, **11**, **13**, **14**, **15**, **16**, **18**, **19**, **21**, **22**, **23**, **27**, **28**.

Cover photograph reproduced with permission of Trevor Clifford.

Every effort has been made to contact copyright holders of any material reproduced in this book. Any omissions will be rectified in subsequent printings if notice is given to the publishers.

Contents

Any words appearing in the text in bold, **like this**,
are explained in the Glossary.

What is bendy?

This toy snake is bendy. You can move its body into many different shapes. Which letter does it make here? (Answer on page 31.)

Some things have to bend to work properly. This girl is trying on a belt. She bends it round her waist and through the buckle.

How bendy?

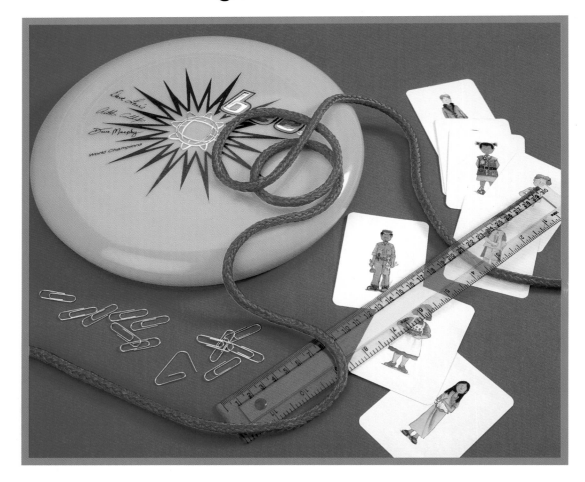

Some things bend more than other things. The playing cards bend more than the ruler. But the rope is the bendiest thing of all in the picture.

These children want to find out whose shoe is the bendiest. They bend each shoe without breaking it. Which shoe is the bendiest? (Answer on page 31.)

What is rigid?

This xylophone is rigid. This means that you cannot change its shape by bending it. However much you push or pull it, it stays the same shape.

The pan and the plate are both rigid. This is just as well! They would be useless if they bent when something heavy was put on them.

How rigid?

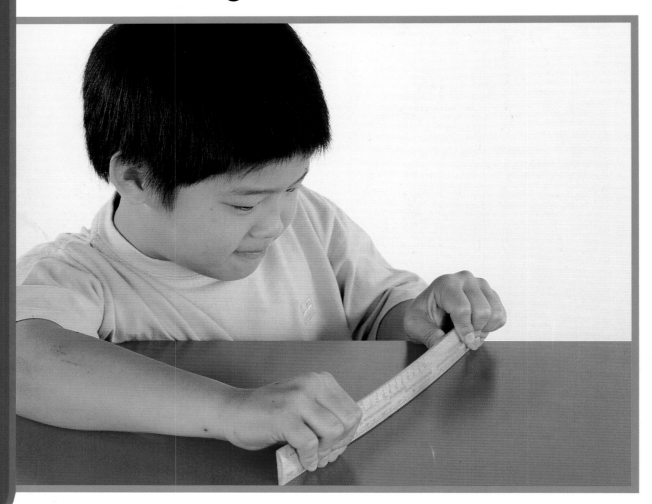

The wooden ruler is quite rigid. It keeps its shape unless you bend it. Even then it only bends a little bit.

The **screwdriver** is more rigid than the wooden ruler. But the most rigid thing in the photo is the tile. The tile does not bend at all.

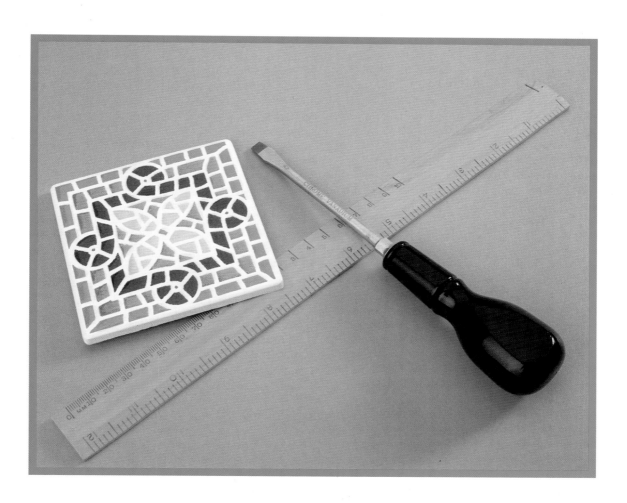

Plastic

Some plastic is bendy. This coat is made of a kind of plastic. Being bendy makes it easier to put on and to move around in.

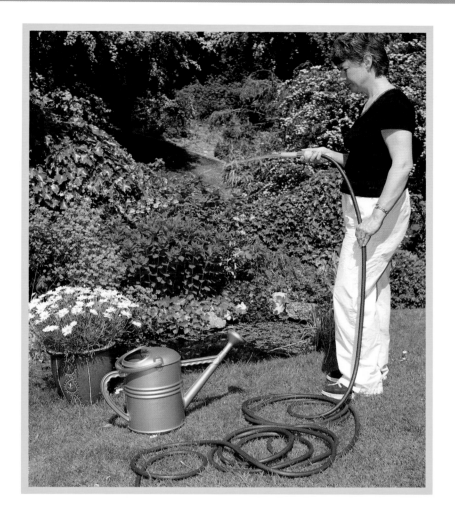

This plastic **hosepipe** is very bendy. It can be wound into a circle when it is not being used. But the plastic watering can is rigid.

Wheels

Bicycle wheels have **rubber** tyres.
Rubber is strong but bendy. It bends
as you go over a bump in the path.

Bicycle wheels have a rigid **rim** and rigid
spokes. The rim and the spokes hold the
wheels in shape. What shape are the
rims in this picture? (Answer on page 31.)

Shoes

Shoes bend as you walk. This allows you to bend your foot. The bottom of a shoe is made of strong plastic or **leather**.

These **clogs** are made of wood. The wood is rigid and does not bend as you walk. It is not very easy to walk in clogs!

Paper and cardboard

A sheet of paper is very bendy. It can be rolled into a tube or folded several times. When you unroll the sheet it becomes flat again.

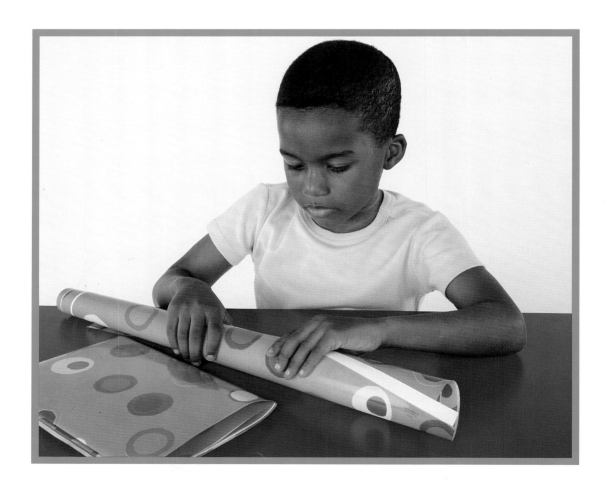

Cardboard is thicker than paper. It is also more rigid than paper. It does not bend easily. Thick cardboard is used to make strong, rigid boxes.

Thick and thin

It is easier to bend something that is thin than something that is thick. These thick **girders** will not bend easily. They make a rigid steel frame.

These paperclips are made of steel, just like the thick girders. But the paperclips are thin. This makes them easy to bend.

Bending and breaking

Most bendy things can only bend so far. Then they break. This woman is bending the stick until it breaks into two pieces.

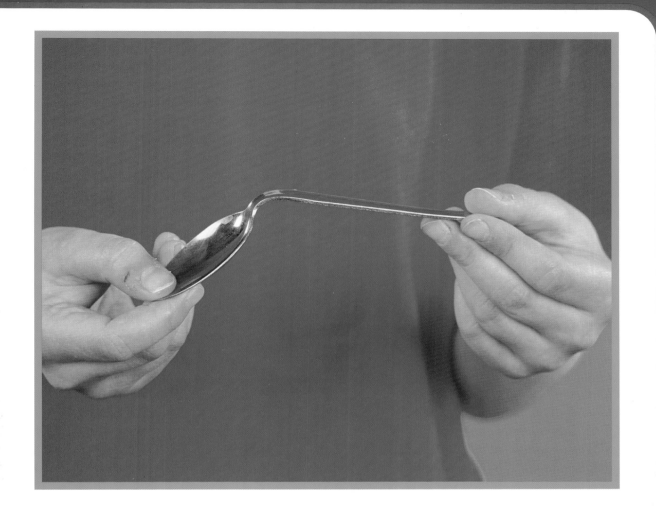

Some things bend and break by mistake. This spoon is bent. If it is bent back and forwards over and over again, the metal will become weaker. Eventually, it will snap in two.

Wood can bend

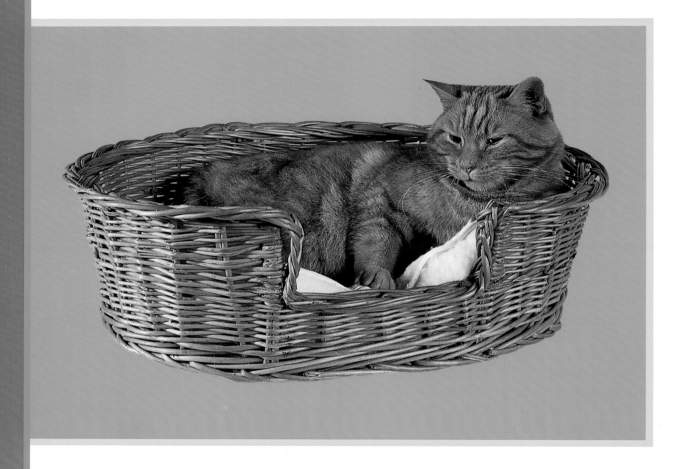

Sometimes wood can bend. This cat's basket is made out of wooden twigs. The twigs are bent and twisted together.

Trees bend when they are blown by strong winds. These palm trees are being bent by the strong winds of a **hurricane**. Bending stops the trees from being blown over.

China is brittle

Rigid things do not bend, but they break. Some rigid things are **brittle**, like these **china** cups and saucers. This means that they crack or break easily.

Plates, mugs, bowls and ornaments are often made of china. Be careful not to drop china! If it is dropped, it may break into many pieces.

Other brittle materials

Glass is even more **brittle** than **china**, especially if it is thin. These glasses are **fragile**. They are made of very fine glass that breaks easily.

Stones and bricks are brittle too. But they are so thick they do not break easily. This worker is using a **sledgehammer** to break up the stone.

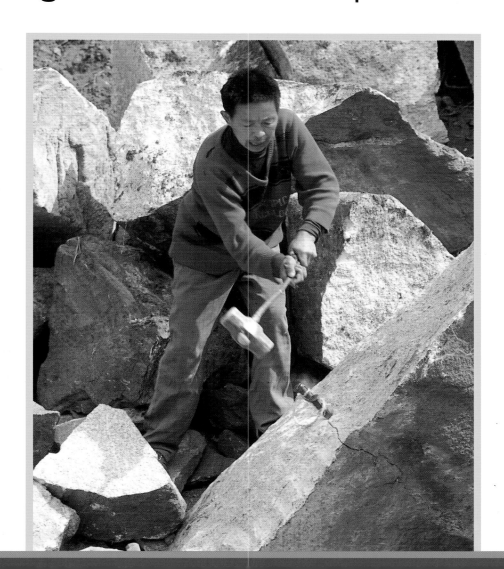

Glossary

brittle easy to break into pieces

china material that is often used to make plates, bowls, cups and vases

clog a shoe with a bottom made of wood

fragile easy to break or to damage

girder a thick piece of steel used to hold up a building

hosepipe a long tube that carries water from a tap

hurricane a storm that includes very strong wind and very heavy rain

leather material made from the skin of a cow or other animal

rim edge

rubber bendy material made from the juice of the rubber tree

screwdriver tool used to screw nails into wood

sledgehammer a big, heavy hammer

spokes set of thin rods that join the **rim** of a wheel to its centre

Answers

page 4
The snake makes the shape of the letter S.

page 7
The girl has the bendiest shoe.

page 15
Each wheel rim makes the shape of a circle.

Index

Titles in the *My World of Science* series include:

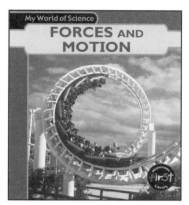

Hardback   0 431 13700 5

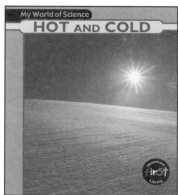

Hardback   0 431 13715 3

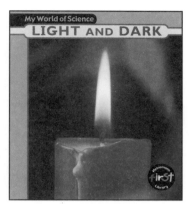

Hardback   0 431 13712 9

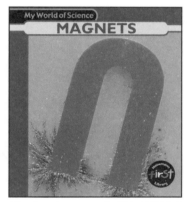

Hardback   0 431 13704 8

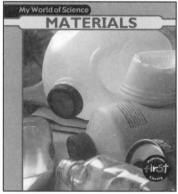

Hardback   0 431 13701 3

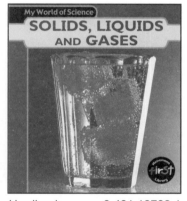

Hardback   0 431 13702 1

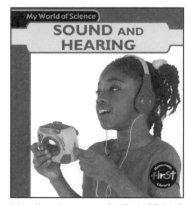

Hardback   0 431 13714 5

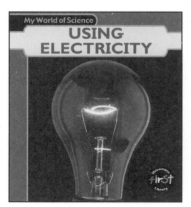

Hardback   0 431 13716 1

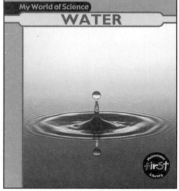

Hardback   0 431 13703 X

Find out about the other titles in this series on our website www.heinemann.co.uk/library